Am I Called?

Basics of the Faith

Am I Called?

How Do We Glorify God?

How Our Children Come to Faith

Is Jesus in the Old Testament?

What Are Election and Predestination?

What Are Spiritual Gifts?

What Happens after Death?

What Is a Reformed Church?

What Is a True Calvinist?

What Is Biblical Preaching?

What Is Church Government?

What Is Discipleship?

What Is Faith?

What Is Grace?

What Is Hell?

What Is Justification by Faith Alone?

What Is Man?

What Is Mercy Ministry?

What Is Perseverance of the Saints?

What Is Providence?

What Is Spiritual Warfare?

What Is the Atonement?

What Is the Christian Worldview?

What Is the Doctrine of Adoption?

What Is the Lord's Supper?

What Is the Trinity?

What Is True Conversion?

What Is Vocation?

What Is Worship Music?

Why Believe in God?

Why Do We Baptize Infants?

Why Do We Have Creeds?

Why Do We Pray?

Why God Gave Us a Book

Sean Michael Lucas, Series Editor

Am I Called?

George W. Robertson

P&R
PUBLISHING
P.O. BOX 817 • PHILLIPSBURG • NEW JERSEY 08865-0817

ISBN: 978-1-59638-543-6 (pbk)
ISBN: 978-1-59638-827-7 (ePub)
ISBN: 978-1-59638-828-4 (Mobi)

Page design by Tobias Design

Printed in the United States of America

Library of Congress Cataloging-in-Publication Data

Robertson, George W. (George William), 1966-
Am I called? / George W. Robertson. -- 1st ed.
pages cm. -- (Basics of the faith)
Includes bibliographical references.
ISBN 978-1-59638-543-6 (pbk.)
1. Clergy--Appointment, call, and election. 2. Vocation, Ecclesiastical.
3. Pastoral theology. I. Title.
BV4011.4.R63 2013
248.8'92--dc23

2012050200

When, at the wise old age of fifteen, I declared that the Lord was calling me to the ministry, my pastor told me, gently but firmly, "Before you say that for sure, you need to know what you are getting yourself into."

In my denomination, a person must receive a call to a particular ministry before he can be approved to serve. Furthermore, the specific terms of that call must be submitted to the governing body of our church. That is the first test of one's call—is one willing to submit to other brethren?

Wesley Benefield understands that test in Clyde Edgerton's novel *Killer Diller.* When Miss Mattie encourages him to become a preacher, he says, "I don't know. I'd have to get ordained. I'm not sure I'd like the ordainers."[1] No one can accept a call until he understands what he is getting himself into and is willing to submit to it as to the Lord. So that is the question—*what is the ministry?*—that must be addressed before we answer what a *call* to the ministry is.

SERVICE

In a word, the ministry is *service*. A pastor's wife recently asked her ninety-eight-year-old husband, a man whom I greatly admire, why he had accepted a call to a new pastorate. "Why can't we just sit in the pew now?" she asked him. The old warrior answered, "Because I came not to be served, but to serve!" (Matt. 20:28).

He had it right. There is only one Head and King of the church, Jesus Christ, who is King over all reality (1 Cor. 15:25; Col. 3:1). Therefore, every minister's authority is only "ministerial" and declarative.[2] A minister labors under the authority of Jesus Christ, who authorizes him to administer the Word to his people through his person and voice. A minister who "lords" over his flock is oxymoronic theologically as well as semantically (1 Peter 5:3). Even the Lord Christ does not wield his authority over the church in a despotic manner. When they are thinking rightly, his subjects submit with joy because they realize the Son of God was humiliated to become their Head (Gal. 4:1–5).

To be a minister of Christ is to be his vicar, to represent him to others, especially through humiliation, trials, and suffering. However, such representation is not mere imitation. To minister vicariously for Christ is to be in union with him. While every Christian is saved only by being united to Christ (Col. 3:3), Paul indicates that there is a peculiar union with Christ in the pastoral ministry. Thus, a minister is an "apostle" (*sent one*) and "priest" only because he is united to Christ (Heb. 3:1). By God's mercy, the gospel minister is privileged to have his life follow the pattern of the Lord's, being physically and emotionally expended on behalf of the people he serves, in order that they might live (2 Cor. 4:1, 11–12). When a pastor asks the Lord for a pattern of ministry, Jesus hands him a towel and a bowl of water and says, "Wash their feet" (John 13:4–14) or a shepherd's crook and says, "Tend my sheep" (John 21:16). When a preacher inquires of Christ how to be promoted in the church, Jesus hands him a cup of suffering (Matt. 20:22).

In turn, the minister's life must become an example of Christ and his redeeming work for the sake of the flock (Phil. 3:17). In her memoir *Leaving Church*, Barbara Brown Taylor put it this way, "Being ordained is not about serving God perfectly but about serving God visibly, allowing other people to learn whatever they can from watching you rise and fall."[3] Even thorny suffering is an act of service to others because through it Christ proves that his "grace is sufficient" to keep the hard-pressed from being "crushed" (2 Cor. 4:7–18; 11:23–30; 12:9).

However, there is a difference in Scripture between being "crushed" (spiritually annihilated) and "bruised" (ministerially prepared) (Isa. 42:3; Matt. 12:20). Bruising is necessary for all Christians to remind them that they are not sufficient without Christ, and the minister especially must be bruised if he will lead his people convincingly to the gospel. Richard Sibbes famously insisted: "No sound whole soul shall ever enter into heaven." Why? Because, as he explained, bruising "makes us more thankful, and, from thankfulness, more fruitful in our lives; for what makes many so cold and barren, but that bruising for sin never endeared God's grace to them?"[4]

The greatest pastors in history were made so by bruising. George Whitefield, not generally known for his pastoral sensitivity, recognized it in Gilbert Tennent, his fellow awakener:

> I never before heard such a searching sermon. He [Gilbert Tennent] convinced me more and more that we can preach the Gospel of Christ no further than we have experienced the power of it in our own hearts. Being deeply convicted of sin, by God's Holy Spirit, at his first conversion, he has learned experimentally to dissect the heart of a natural man. Hypocrites must either soon be converted or enraged at his preaching. He is a son of thunder, and does not fear the faces of men.[5]

Andrew Bonar made a similar observation of Robert Murray M'Cheyne: "This soul was prepared for the awful work of the ministry by much prayer and much study of the word of God, by inward trials, by experience of the depth of corruption in his own heart, and by discoveries of the Savior's fullness of grace."[6]

SERVICE IN PREACHING

But the ministry is not generic service; it is the ministry of the gospel, the specific terms of which are written down in Scripture. Those terms may be gathered up in two big baskets: preaching and pastoring.

Preaching is the minister's most important duty. In fact, it is arguably the most important task in the world, because the lost cannot (ordinarily) hear the message of salvation without "someone preaching to them" (Rom. 10:14–15). This also clarifies that the pastor must not make an artificial distinction between "personal evangelism" and "pulpit preaching." This seems to be the apostle's point when Paul bookends his charge to his young student in 2 Timothy 4:1–5 with the commands to "preach the word" at the beginning and "do the work of an evangelist" at the end.

Reinforcing the eternal significance attached to preaching, the Westminster Shorter Catechism answers question 89, "How is the Word made effectual to salvation?", in this way: "The Spirit of God maketh the reading, *but especially the preaching*, of the Word, an effectual means of convincing and converting sinners, and of building them up in holiness and comfort, through faith, unto salvation." If preaching is so important, and much more than merely reading the text, then what is it? Preaching requires a minister who has sufficiently studied God's Word (Ezra 7:10) so that he can explain its meaning and apply it to people's lives (Neh. 8:8, 12) in a way that leads them to Jesus Christ as the fulfillment of all Scripture (Luke 24:25–27; 2 Tim. 4:5).

As a gift from the Spirit, true preaching reinforces the fact that God's grace is accentuated by the weakness of the minister. Paul told his Corinthian critics that God proved his power and wisdom through the "foolishness" of preaching to save (1 Cor. 1:21). Perhaps it is because preaching seems to be such an unlikely force for advancing the kingdom that God identifies it as among the "greater gifts" to be desired (1 Cor. 12:31; cf. Eph. 4:11–16). While every elder of the church is to be "able to teach" (2 Tim. 2:24), those who are especially marked out for "double honor" (is that triple honor?) are those whose "work is preaching and teaching" (1 Tim. 5:17).

While preaching is not as impressive as speaking in an unknown tongue, which Paul was apparently able to do as well, he preferred to preach a few "intelligible words" than many more words that wowed. Why? Because the first requirement for preaching is to study the Word *in order* to instruct (1 Cor. 14:19). This also explains Paul's strong charge to his spiritual son, Timothy. Paul told this young pastor in Ephesus to "preach the Word . . . in season and out of season" in such a clear way that faithful ones who heard him could in turn "teach others" (2 Tim. 4:2 and 2:2).

Therefore, preaching first requires a prepared man who is able to explain the Scriptures to those who listen. The apostles' peculiar power to teach and preach gave evidence that they were "unschooled, ordinary men who had been with Jesus" (Acts 4:2, 13). That is, they had been prepared by him to explain the Scriptures. Even the greater apostle Paul, though selectively schooled by Greek and Jewish scholars, had to go to Jesus' seminary for three years before he was ready to preach the gospel (Gal. 1:17–18).

While there may be many ways to get prepared, preparation in knowledge and experience is essential to preaching. The brilliant and powerful Scottish preacher Alexander Whyte said of preparation for preaching: "If I were choosing a minister for myself and could not have both the book-knowledge and the experience of the Christian life in one and the same man . . . I would say that, much as I like an able and learned sermon from and able and learned man, I would rather have less learning and more experience."[7]

The second requirement for preaching is to apply the Scriptures in such a way that those who hear look to Jesus as their pattern and power for doing what God calls them to be and do. After hearing Ezra preach, the people responded appropriately—repenting, rejoicing, reconciling, restoring. The apostles' preaching "turned the world upside down" (Acts 17:6). By that expression, critics meant that the application of the Scriptures changed cultural norms, worship patterns, and family dynamics. However, the laws and regulations were not new. They had been around in Israel since Mt. Sinai and even since the foundation of the world. These old laws became newly transformative because the reason for them was clearly proclaimed, namely, the grace of God in the person and work of Jesus Christ. The apostles turned the world upside down by preaching from the same Bible Jesus had, the only Bible at the time, the Old Testament Scriptures that had also been the Bible of Ezra (Acts 17:3).

Paul laconically summarized preaching with these words: "Him we proclaim" (Col. 1:28). If there is no preaching without a prepared man explaining the Scriptures, then there is no Christian preaching without demonstrating how Christ motivates and enables us to obey every command of Scripture.

Some congregations prefer legalism because it can provide a false sense of security that leads to pride. Jonathan Parsons was a pastor in Lyme, Connecticut, when the First Great Awakening occurred. After his own conversion, he began preaching Christ—to the great consternation of his proud congregation. The criticism so wore on him that he confessed, "I was awfully deserted of God, and got into a very dull, legal frame myself; and then some were better pleased." Eventually the gospel gained ascendancy in his life again, and he returned to preaching Christ as the end of all the Scriptures and the one who enables us to obey all its instructions.[8]

Only Christ-centered preaching can reform behavior in a way that produces a long, grateful, genuine, and joyful obedience. Richard Sibbes was a typical Puritan who knew how to apply the healing power of the gospel to "bruised reeds" (the title of his most famous book). Observe it in this moving testimony from one of his parishioners:

> I was for three years together wounded for sins, and under a sense of my corruptions, which were many; and I followed sermons, pursuing the means, and was constant in duties and doing; looking for heaven that way. And then I was so precise for outward formalities, that I censured all to be reprobates, that wore their hair anything long, and not short above their ears; or that wore great ruffs, and gorgets, or fashions, and follies. But yet I was distracted in my mind, wounded in conscience, and wept often and bitterly, and prayed earnestly, but yet had no comfort, till I heard that sweet saint . . . Doctor Sibbs, by whose means and ministry I was brought to peace and joy in my spirit. His sweet soul-melting Gospel-sermons won my heart and refreshed me much, for by him I saw and had much of God and was confident in Christ, and could overlook the world. . . . My heart held firm and resolved and my desires all heaven-ward.[9]

Preaching—the minister's most important duty—requires that he be sufficiently prepared in God's Word by knowledge and experience so that he can explain its meaning and apply it to people's lives in a way that leads them to Jesus Christ as the fulfillment of all Scripture.

SERVICE IN PASTORING

The second privileged duty of a gospel minister is pastoring God's people. However, this order should not convey that pastoring is distantly second in importance to preaching. As Phillips Brooks said, "The preacher who is not a pastor grows remote; the pastor who is not a preacher grows petty."[10]

The difficulty of capturing all that is included in the biblical portrait of a good pastor is illustrated by the various outlines writers have used. My mentor, Don MacNair, used the acronym GOES (Guardian, Overseer, Example, Shepherd).[11] Professor Tim Witmer describes the task as knowing, feeding, leading, and protecting.[12] For clarity, I will be less metaphorical and say that the pastor's responsibilities include leading in worship and praying for the people.

With language rooted in the gospel itself, Paul urged the Ephesian elders to be "shepherds of the church of God, which he bought with his own blood" (Acts 20:28). The pattern for such shepherding was established early in the book of Acts by the apostles when they exhorted the church to elect seven deacons to attend to the needs of the Grecian widows. Insisting that they could not do both, the leaders said that they must focus on not only the "ministry of the word" but also "prayer" (Acts 6:4). In the Greek text, there is a definite article before "prayer" (*the* prayer), apparently a shorthand reference for the whole worship service over which the apostles were stewards.

These men understood that worship is critically important for the right shepherding of their flock, because the Spirit specially works in a properly crafted worship service. Believers are encouraged and instructed (1 Cor. 14:6). At other times their errant beliefs are corrected (Ps. 73:17). Still others can be severely chastised for irreverence (1 Cor. 11:30). The Spirit also works evangelistically to convince the unbeliever that God is really among his people (1 Cor. 14:25). But none of these effects of the gospel is possible unless Christ is at the center of the worship service. And who better to ensure that Christ is at the center than the one whose sacred responsibility it is to preach Christ?

What is required for the proper crafting of a worship service? A worship service is properly crafted as Bryan Chapell says, when it "recapitulates the gospel."[13] Although other gifted ones will assist him, the pastor ensures that the gospel is presented in every worship service by syntax and structure. As he leads his people through the various movements of the worship service, he can point out with his verbal transitions the good news in the hymns and prayers and Scripture readings. But he should also structure the service in such a way that worshipers are reminded of how they came to Christ and continue in him. So the pastor calls people to worship as God calls them to Christ. Worshipers praise God for his call and invoke his presence. They confess their sins and hear God's pardoning grace through Christ. After assurance of forgiveness, they boldly come into the Father's presence through prayer, knowing that the Spirit intercedes for them. Then the Word is applied so that they might respond in grateful obedience. Finally, they depart with God's blessing.

Even more special is the ministry of the sacraments in worship. Augustine called baptism and the Lord's Supper "visible words."[14] Nothing within the sacraments is magical, but the presence of Christ is real. The sacraments remind worshipers that a kind heavenly Father, knowing his children's human frailty, desires to touch their consciences in an objective way to assure their faith and increase their love for one another.

As an extension of the preaching of God's saving grace, baptism reminds the worshiper that the Spirit continually cleanses from sin (Col. 2:11–12; 1 Peter 3:21). As an extension of the pastor's preaching God's keeping grace, the Lord's Supper reminds the faithful that all God's promises are fulfilled in Christ (Luke 22:15–20; 1 Cor. 11:27–30). Revivalist Gilbert Tennent passionately preached the connection between the grace of God and its confirmation in the Lord's Supper:

> Seeing God has justify'd us freely, without good Works, we should express our Thankfulness to him, by a more

> cheerful, sincere and steady Practice of them, to which let the Love of God constrain us. And particularly, let justify'd Persons obey their Lords command, in sitting down at his Table, and Commemorating his dying Love. . . O Sirs! It is the Exercise of a justifying Faith, which as an Eye, can only help us to behold our Lord's Sufferings in a right Manner; and, as a Conduit, can convey to us the Benefits of them.[15]

The gospel minister must carefully steward the sacraments as an extension of his ministry of the Word for the benefit of God's flock. Such stewardship includes the pastor's sobering responsibility to discipline persistent wayward members of the church. Since baptism and the Lord's Supper are privileges afforded to those who have been publicly recognized as adherents to the gospel preached, those who disavow that profession with their words and actions forfeit those privileges through formal church discipline. The Westminster Confession of Faith (30.2) articulates the minister's authorization to extend or withhold gospel benefits as he follows the protocol of Scripture:

> To these officers the keys of the kingdom are committed; by virtue whereof, they have power, respectively, to retain and remit sins; to shut that kingdom against the impenitent, both by the Word, and censures; and to open it unto penitent sinners, by the ministry of the Gospel; and by absolution from censures, as occasion shall require.

Everyone agrees that a good pastor knows his people. He cannot be a vicar of the Good Shepherd without "knowing his sheep" (John 10:26–27). Neither can he claim to follow in the footsteps of the apostles who organized the early church to care for widows (Acts 6:1–7), comforted the afflicted (2 Cor. 1:3–11), wept for the wayward

(2 Cor. 2:4), pleaded for reconciliation (Phil. 4:2), watched over the flock (1 Peter 5:2), and looked after orphans and widows (James 1:27). As Alexander Whyte said, "Watching for the souls of our people, one by one, day in and day out,—that, above everything else, that, and nothing else,—makes any man a pastor of the apostolic type."[16] Similarly, the nineteenth-century Scottish elder David Dickson challenged pastors and elders in this way:

> He must be acquainted with them all, old and young, their history, their occupations, their habits, their ways of thinking. They and their children should be their personal friends, so that they naturally turn to him as to one on whom they can depend as a kind and sympathizing friend and a faithful counselor.[17]

However, knowledge of his people is not the end of the pastor's work; he knows them *in order* to pray for them. When a pastor knows his people well, he is able to apply the Word he preaches to them. However, that Word preached will lack power unless it is accompanied by the prayers of their loving shepherd:

> Understanding and memory and industry must all be sanctified by secret prayer many times every day, and then laid out every day in the instruction, impression, and comfort of his people. And, then, that privileged people will be as happy in possessing that man for their minister as the sheep of Immanuel's Land were in having Knowledge set over them for their shepherd. They will never look up without being fed.[18]

Prayer never comes naturally; it is a duty to which Christians must always be called because it is contrary to our flesh (Matt. 26:41). This is no less true of a sinner who happens to be a minister of the gospel. While all Christians are kings and priests, the minister has a particular royal and priestly responsibility to intercede lovingly for his people in response to the Chief Shepherd who loved him first (Rev. 1:5–6). As Pascal said, by giving us the tool of prayer, God extends to us the "dignity of causality." Commenting on that incredible privilege to participate in the causation of God's will on behalf of others, Alexander Whyte says:

> And the magnificence of all true prayer—its nobility, its royalty, its absolute divinity—all stand in this, that it is the greatest kind of act and office that man, or angel, can ever enter on and perform. Earth is at its very best; and heaven is at its very highest, when men and angels magnify their office of prayer and of praise before the throne of God.[19]

In his high priestly prayer, Christ prayed, "For them I sanctify myself" (John 17:19). Even the Son of God set himself apart in order to intercede for us (Heb. 7:25; 9:24). Carrying on his work, the apostles likewise prayed earnestly on behalf of those for whom they were responsible (Acts 9:40; Rom. 10:1; 2 Cor. 13:7; Eph. 1:16; Col. 1:9; Philem. 6; 3 John 2). In fact, so essential is prayer to the ministry as Christ and his apostles exemplify it to be that one cannot consider himself a minister of the gospel without a devotion to it. Christian author Flannery O'Connor once described a prayerless minister as "one part minister and three parts masseuse."[20] Eugene Peterson says even more bluntly: The pastor who does not pray as well as preach is an "embarrassment."[21]

SERVICE IN CALLING

Now that we have explored what the ministry is in terms of preaching and pastoring, we cannot ignore a basic question: What is a *calling* to ministry? In the Old and the New Testaments, both the call and response are initiated and enabled by God's grace (Rom. 8:28–30; 9:11). When God calls creation, a person, or a people, his call is always to a certain task that will serve redemptive ends. Calling light "day" and darkness "night," calling the expanse "sky" and the dry ground "land" was more than taxonomy. God was commissioning these parts of his creation as actors in the divine redemptive drama. Paul explains that God "created all things. His intent was that now, through the church, the manifold wisdom of God should be made known" (Eph. 3:9–10). Creation was called to be the arena of redemption tangibly reflecting what God is doing with the people he is saving (Jer. 31:35; 33:19–22, 25–26; Rom. 8:22–23).

The Creator also calls his people corporately to imitate his grace before the world. In the Old Testament, his people were called to demonstrate to the world the fullness of the life Yahweh's laws bring (Deut. 4:5–9). He called them to observe special days and dietary practices to prove that they were a holy people set apart to the Lord (Lev. 23:2–3; Num. 28:25). Their calling to live in loving obedience was to exemplify that they were specially called from hopelessness and the far reaches of the world to be righteous representatives of God's holy name (Isa. 41:9; 42:6; 43:1; Ezek. 16:1–7). Likewise, in the New Testament, God's people must recognize their once-lost condition outside Christ and acknowledge the implicit call made on a believer's life by gracious gifts like peace, hope, and heaven (Rom. 1:7; 1 Cor. 1:2, 9; 7:15; Eph. 4:1, 4; Phil. 3:13–14).

The Redeemer also calls individuals to redemptive tasks. When God called to Adam, "Where are you?" he summoned him out of his rebellion and shame into gracious restoration and recommissioned him as an image bearer in the creation (Gen. 3:9, 15, 21–24). The commission to take dominion over all the earth is one still incumbent on every believer, imbuing every legitimate vocation with holiness. Christians are each directly responsible to their Lord for bringing the kingdom of God to bear within their social stations and vocations (1 Cor. 7:17–23). Outward circumstances are irrelevant, as are the accolades or abuses of others, as long as one's calling is performed as an act of worship before a gracious King.

Even civic leaders are expected to answer the Sovereign One's call worshipfully. Paralyzed by fear that he did not have sufficient strength, Saul had to be called from "among the supplies" to be Israel's first king. No professed servant of God should be found cowering among the baggage, so unlike King Jesus (1 Sam. 10:22). In contrast, though David was profoundly flawed, he looked to the Lord all his days for the strength to be the great king of Israel through whose line his Greater Son would come (1 Sam. 16:9, 10; Ps. 110:1).

Still others are called by no inherent worthiness but entirely by God's mercy to exercise particular leadership in the advancement of the kingdom through the priestly and prophetic ministry of the Word, sacraments, and prayer (2 Cor. 4:1). Abraham was called to establish the beachhead in the land, which would see the fulfillment of God's promises in Christ (Gen. 12:1). Moses was called to lead the children of Israel out of their bondage in Egypt and back to the Promised Land (Ex. 3:4, 10). Samuel was called to restore the priesthood in Israel and provide a pattern of that great Priest to come (1 Sam. 3:1–14).

Prophets were called to point ahead to the Word, which would become flesh, and to apply its implications to their contemporaries (Amos 7:15; Jonah 1:1). Some were called to dramatize the warnings they prophesied to God's wayward people, as when Isaiah walked about stripped and barefoot for three years (Isa. 20:4) or when Ezekiel lay on his side for 390 days (Ezek. 4) or when Jeremiah wore a yoke of wood and leather (Jer. 27; 28) or when Hosea married a prostitute (Hosea 1:2). Some men were called from their mother's wombs to be prophetic messengers of the Word that makes hearers wise for salvation (Jer. 1:14–19; Luke 1:45; 2 Tim. 3:15). The eternal significance of every calling, especially that of the gospel ministry, must move the true servant-leader to "call on the name of the Lord" in private prayer and corporate worship (Gen. 4:26; 1 Kings 18:24; Ps. 116:17; Joel 2:32).

But how does an individual know he is called to the gospel ministry? The biblical theology of calling and response above contains the basic answer—by the Word and prayer in the context of a worshiping community. Clarity in discerning God's will begins with a heart that is willing to be led. Willingness to be led by the Lord is a mark of wisdom, and wisdom begins with the "fear of the Lord" (Prov. 1:7). The relationship between the fear of the Lord and answering God's call can be observed in the dramatic growth of Abraham's faith. Throughout Genesis 12–21, Abraham is hardly the paragon of faith and obedience. Though he was called from Ur to go to the Promised Land, he apparently got bogged down in Haran and had to be called again (Gen. 12:1). After arriving in Canaan, he panicked over famine and ran to Egypt (12:10). While there, he lied about the identity of his wife to protect himself, a sin he later repeated among the Philistines (12:12–20; 20:1–18). He sought to manipulate God's promises by producing an heir through a surrogate mother (16:1–16), whom he later cruelly drove into the desert (21:1–21).

However, Abraham's responsiveness to the Lord's direction changed dramatically by chapter 22, when God called him to sacrifice his only covenant son. Without a word, Abraham made the preparations and with counterintuitive faith concluded that God would raise Isaac from the dead (Heb. 11:19). What happened in Abraham's heart to explain such readiness to do the Lord's bidding? The angel of the Lord revealed it: "Now I know that you fear God" (Gen. 22:12). While it is true that fear sometimes means fright in the Bible, it does not always connote a servile attitude. In this case, it can be nothing other than the dread of disappointing a father coupled with deep trust in a covenant-keeping God in whom all his promises are "yes and amen" in Jesus. John Murray called Abraham's fear an example of an "all-pervasive God-consciousness conditioned by a covenant-consciousness."[22] Abraham heard God's call clearly and answered obediently because his heart was confident in God's promises. That trust in God's sovereign grace produced wisdom that made him willing to obey. Discerning God's call should begin with fixing one's heart on the Christ in whom all things hold together (Col. 1:17).

God never fails to get his man. He does not wring his hands in heaven, wondering if anyone is going to answer his call to the ministry. "The one who calls you is faithful, and he will do it" (1 Thess. 5:24). The man who wrote these words knew this as well as anyone—when God had decided it was time for Saul to become Paul, apostle to the Gentiles, Saul had been stopped in his tracks by a voice from heaven and a blinding light. Elijah, Jonah, Habakkuk, Peter, and John Mark all had moments when they thought God ran a volunteer army. But each was captured by God's lovingkindness and redeployed as an emissary of the gospel.

The wise auditor of God will also be willing to receive direction iteratively rather than all at once. When David was fleeing from Saul, God called him to attack the Philistines, who were oppressing the people of Keilah, and promised to give him victory. However, when David asked if the liberated citizens would betray him and if Saul would pursue him, God answered laconically, "They will" and "He will." Without complete knowledge of how God would protect him, David kept moving forward because he believed the God who promised ultimate victory (1 Sam. 23:1–29). Likewise, the servant of God must follow God's call even if it feels like leaping from one rock to another across a swiftly moving river, unable to see more than one rock ahead.

Evangelist Harry Ironside related a personal testimony he heard from the great preacher of Westminster Chapel, G. Campbell Morgan. Soon after Morgan resigned from his job as a schoolmaster to pursue the ministry, he had a crisis of faith. On the night he was set apart to his call, he felt he could hear the Lord asking this question, "Now, Morgan, you have been set apart definitely for the ministry of the Word. Do you want to be a great preacher, or do you want to be my servant?"

Morgan confessed to Ironside that at first he thought, "Oh, I want to be a great preacher; surely there is no more laudable ambition than that." But then he thought, "Why should the Lord put it that way? Why can I not be his servant and a great preacher?" His soul struggled to answer the question because he realized that he might be called to some obscure ministry if he asked to be a servant. Eventually the Spirit got the victory in his heart, and he exclaimed one day, "O blessed Lord, I would rather be thy servant than anything else!" Ironside concluded his recollection this way, "And God not only made him His servant but a great preacher. Sometimes we fulfil our deepest ambition by foregoing our own desires and saying, 'Lord, I want to be Thy servant; just take me, make me, break me, do what Thou wilt with me.' "[23]

David consulted the priestly ephod to discern God's will (1 Sam. 23:9). Elsewhere, the Bible calls this priestly garment the Urim and Thummim (Ex. 28:30). While we are not sure how it worked exactly, it basically gave yes or no answers. Someone seeking God's call may wish for such an instrument today. However, we must understand that the Bible is far better because in it God gives reasons for doing what he requires rather than just giving commands.

A classic example is Romans 12:1–2, which calls us to surrender our bodies as living sacrifices to God only after describing over the course of eleven chapters the breathtaking nature of God's grace in Christ. That total bodily surrender includes the mind, which Paul promises will be transformed by God's Word. We are assured that we will be able to "test and approve what God's will is" (v. 2). Therefore, when we hear promises of our inseparability from Christ's love, it moves us to a joyful submission, which results in clear direction. To put oneself willingly in God's hands to be led by him is to embark on a journey that will consummate in one's gradual transformation into the likeness of Christ (Col. 1:6). Paul assured the young pastor Timothy that in contrast to those who "will not get very far" (2 Tim. 3:9), the man of God will always be "thoroughly equipped for every good work" by the "Holy Scriptures which are able to make you wise for salvation" (2 Tim. 3:9, 14–17). With a heart trusting his faithful Father, the man who wants to hear if God is calling him to minister must listen carefully to God's Word as he reads it and hears it preached.

Bible reading is incomplete without prayers for the Spirit to illuminate the Word. The one waiting on the Lord's call must prayerfully open his heart before the Lord so that the Spirit will apply the Scriptures in ways he uniquely needs. The Spirit, working by and with the Word, will do so because, as Augustine said, the Word "finds us."[24]

This is how the first missionaries were called in Acts 13. Luke notes that there were "prophets and teachers" in the church at Antioch (v. 1). In other words, the Word was being faithfully preached and taught. With the Word as the foundation of their worship, the men were prayerfully seeking God's guidance, even fasting so as to focus their minds and time on hearing from the Lord. It was "while" this prayerful study of God's Word in worship was occurring that the "Holy Spirit said, 'Set apart for me Barnabas and Saul for the work to which I have called them' " (v. 2). In Edmund Clowney's classic book on this topic, he wrote, "It is quite possible to overestimate the gifts you have: it is quite impossible to over-supplicate the gifts you need."[25]

DISCERNING GIFTS FOR SERVICE

Knowing whether a man is truly called to the ministry is critically important both because of the peculiar difficulties of the ministry (2 Cor. 4:7–12) and because of the stricter judgment he will be subjected to as a minister of the Word (James 3:1). While every calling and vocation is ultimately from God and dignified by him for his kingdom purposes, the truth remains that the call to gospel ministry is the highest one in terms of God's peculiar use of it to extend his kingdom. It must take precedence in a man's life over all other possibilities. As Clowney said, "Men with the gifts for the ministry have the capacity for success in other fields, but they are not free to choose them. God's first command still stands: man is to replenish the earth and subdue it; but the Great Commission takes priority over it."[26] Furthermore, the minister must have a clear conviction of his calling so that he can give an answer to his doubting conscience and other gainsayers during dark days of ministry. He must be able to answer with Jeremiah that he is only running on this all-important errand because God sent him (Jer. 23:21).

After understanding, however broadly, what a minister does, the one exploring a call must examine himself to see if he (1) aspires to be a pastor and (2) has the spiritual gifts to be a pastor. Paul affirms aspiration as one means of determining a call when he says, "Whoever aspires to be an overseer desires a noble task" (1 Tim. 3:1). There is nothing unspiritual about desiring to be a minister of the gospel.

So how should one determine how strong those desires are? Spiritual gifts analyses and personality assessments like DISC and Meyers-Briggs are useful for self-examination. In recent years, former Gallup pollster Marcus Buckingham has made a helpful contribution toward discerning one's calling by encouraging people to discover their strengths rather than obsess on their weaknesses. I have used his SIGN acronym to help many men discern not only their initial calling, but also subsequent callings. Buckingham suggests that people keep a "strong week" list as an experiment: a piece of paper divided in the middle with a list of experiences "loved" on one side and "loathed" on the other. Those experiences "loved" should meet the following criteria: proved *successful*, revealed an *instinct*, inspired *growth*, and fulfilled a *need*. By "instinct," Buckingham means something a person looks forward to and anticipates with eagerness. By "growth," he refers to a refreshing expenditure of energy: an activity that not only challenges but also strengthens. "Need" is that subjective sense of deep satisfaction after an achievement, even if it was exhausting. Buckingham warns, however, that it is possible to experience growth, instinct, and need and still not be successful. Someone might *feel* successful, but more objective observers might judge differently. It is also possible for someone to feel like a failure, only to be assured by others that he has succeeded.

There are two problems, however, with relying entirely on personality tests and self-examination when determining a call to the ministry. One I already mentioned: people can misjudge their own success. The other is that there is no single personality type necessary to being a minister of the gospel.

It has been common, at least in the West, to assume that a leader of any kind must be an extrovert. In his textbook on leadership, Richard Daft calls extroversion one of the "Big Five personality dimensions" necessary to success.[27] However, in recent years researchers like Jim Collins have challenged this prejudice. In fact, in *Good to Great*, Collins demonstrated that showy, high-profile leaders can actually hinder the long-term health of an organization.[28]

The Bible well illustrates the fact that God uses a range of personality types to minister the good news to the Everyman. Noah was brave but inconsistent. Abraham was cowardly and intuitive. Elijah had emotional highs and lows. Jeremiah was sensitive and depressive. Jonah was stubborn and bold. Peter was outspoken and impulsive. Luke was methodical and self-effacing. Paul was brilliant and judgmental. The Lord powerfully used each of these very different men as ministers of the Word to advance his kingdom. He harnessed their strengths to pull his purposes, and he made obvious the grace of his strength in their pronounced weaknesses (2 Cor. 12:9). So the question of one's potential call to the ministry is never, "Do I have the personality for it?" but "Does God want to use me, with my unique blend of personality traits, as the vessel through which to communicate the gospel vocationally?" Knowing one's personality traits will always be helpful in guiding one's approach to ministry, but those traits must never be the final determination of one's qualification or disqualification for gospel service.

Another problem with determining one's call based on a private subjective analysis is that such analysis can misjudge success. The Spirit guides individuals toward their calling through the officers and community of the church. An Old Testament prophet's word was only believed to come from the Lord if it fit with previous revelation and if the faith community observed signs fulfilling it (Deut. 13:1–5; 18:20; 28:22). Though Paul had been called dramatically on the road to Emmaus, he had to submit his right understanding of the gospel to the apostles in Jerusalem (Gal. 2:9). The early church discerned who was Judas's apostolic successor (Acts 1:23) and later who were qualified to serve the widows as deacons (Acts 6:3). Elders were elected (Acts 14:23; cf. Acts 20:28). And Paul reminded the timid Timothy that the church and her elders had recognized his gifts and set him apart for the ministry (1 Tim. 4:14; 2 Tim. 1:6).

Therefore, the one who wishes to know if he is called to the ministry must submit himself to the counsel of his pastors and elders as well as the scrutiny of the local congregation where he is trying out his gifts (1 Cor. 14:29, 31). If he is being lovingly shepherded in his church, his spiritual fathers and mothers, sisters and brothers will reflect to him where his gifts are being successfully deployed and where they are not (Eph. 4:11–16). As he lives in humble reliance on the Spirit's direction, he will not be self-promoting but instead amazed at and thankful for the Lord's work through him.

Wycliffe pioneer L. L. Legters was once staying with a friend who said of a pastor in town, "That man can't preach at all, but he is the meekest man I ever saw." Shortly thereafter, Mr. Legters asked the pastor if he thought he was a meek man. The pastor's eyes welled up with tears as he said, "How I have prayed that God would make me meek, but no one knows the stiffness of my neck or the hardness of my heart."[29] Others will sometimes better recognize the Spirit's gifts in us than we do ourselves.

What then should a man be doing among God's people in order to be observed and counseled? Having observed how the church has typically recognized her ministers, I can say, "More of what he has already been doing spontaneously." That is Ed Clowney's basic thesis in *Called to the Ministry*:

> The buying-up of opportunities that shapes all Christian service has peculiar importance in the case of a man called to the gospel ministry. Since your calling is determined at last by your gifts, you prove your calling as you improve your gifts. . . . God's call *to* service normally comes *in* service. Begin with prayer. Unless your service is a living sacrifice, you cannot please God. But don't stop with prayer. Your calling will be clear as God's blessing crowns your words and deeds for him.[30]

Ordination is the church's authorization for a man to do what he has already been doing—at least categorically. It means that, at least in some general way, a would-be minister is teaching the Word and shepherding people in a manner the church views as effective. Ordination only officially commissions the man to do more of the same at a higher level of accountability; it does not magically supply what is not already present organically in his daily life.

SERVICE IN CONFIRMING THE CALL

After information, insights, and feedback have been gathered about a man's fitness for gospel ministry, a decision must be made. Assuming everything indicates that he is called to the ministry and has met all the training requirements in his branch of the church, the man must finally obey. This action is ordinarily a response to an internal call by the Spirit confirmed by an external call by his church.

In an excursus to his commentary on Revelation 1:19–20, the Covenanter James Durham of Glasgow provided rare wisdom to help a candidate for ordination (ordinand) to answer the internal and external call to the ministry. He explained that God tailors the balance of the internal and external according to a man's emotional composition. That is, if someone is receiving less external confirmation by pastors, elders, and congregation, the internal impulse of the Spirit will be stronger. Conversely, if one is naturally inclined to caution, the external draw will be stronger. Durham helpfully added that in the case of a more cautious person, God will "draw the person by steps, who might otherwise be scared, if all were presented to him together."[31]

That "secret instinct" of the Spirit (as John Calvin might call it) [32] can be identified by six characteristics, which Durham described and which I will try to put in more contemporary terms. First, the Spirit's leading may be discerned by increased rationality and peace. Second, while the Spirit directs the mind, he enables the will to obey even if obedience is counterintuitive. Third, the manner of the Spirit's leadership reflects his ultimate goal, which is the promotion of God's glory and the edification of God's people. Fourth, the Spirit leads "kindly" in accordance with the Scriptures—as opposed to the Devil who "drives the heart violently"—so that one desires to respond to grace. Fifth, the Spirit never contradicts the means of grace but rather leads through Scripture and prayer. Finally, the Spirit never leads one to ministry without also providing the appropriate gifts.[33] Clowney affirms this last point especially, "The particular service a man is called to give is determined by the gifts he has received (Rom. 12:3–8). . . . *The call of the Word of God to the gospel ministry comes to ALL those who have the gifts for such a ministry.*"[34]

When a candidate senses the concurrence of these motions within his mind and heart, he may be sure that it is the Spirit of

Christ and not the Spirit of the Age who is leading him to answer God's call to gospel ministry.

Not only is the internal impulse necessary, but an external call from the church ordinarily confirms a man's calling. Sometimes this occurs at the initiation of the candidate, who, being moved internally with an affection for ministry, approaches his church leaders and asks for their confirmation. That was the case with Paul, who went up to Jerusalem to submit himself to the apostolic pillars of the church (Gal. 2:9).

In my ecclesiastical tradition, a man who senses a call will first approach the elders of his local church, who take him "under care" after interviewing him for his sense of internal call along with a testimony to its external confirmation through the exercise of his gifts. They then recommend him to come under the presbytery, a more regional association of elders, which observes and evaluates his "deportment, diligence, and progress in study" during his formal preparation.[35] As he grows in his knowledge and passes oral and written exams, the candidate is licensed to preach regularly. When he receives a specific call from a church, he stands for further tests of his personal character and knowledge before he is finally ordained.

At other times, the leaders of the church, recognizing the Spirit's gifting of a man, may press him despite his reluctance to answer a call to ministry. One can infer that it was Paul and Peter's practice to pursue men whom they perceived were gifted for ministry. It appears Paul recruited Timothy and Titus, and Peter urged elders to shepherd the flock "because you are willing" (1 Peter 5:2). Historically, the church has often pressed into service gifted but reluctant candidates. As Durham points out, even though Ambrose was an unbaptized Roman senator, the church unanimously elected him to be Bishop of Milan.[36] His preaching of the gospel was so powerful that it took down the strongholds of Augustine's intellectual objections to Christianity.

Durham further illustrated from his tough Scottish church's *Book of Discipline* the sometimes very active role a church body may take in issuing a call to a stubborn prophet:

> Moreover men in whom is supposed to be any Gift, which might edify the Church, if they were employed, must be charged by the Ministers and Elders to join themselves with the Session and company of interpreters, to the end that the Kirk may judge wither they be able to serve to God's glory and the profit of the Kirk, in the vocation of Ministers or not. And, if any be found disobedient, and not willing to communicate the Gifts and special graces of God with their brethren, after sufficient admonition, Discipline must proceed against them.[37]

While such a threat may offend our contemporary sensibilities, it reminds us that God's call to ministry is an eternally significant demand and not one vocational option among many. Where would the church be if William Farel had not issued the threat to Calvin, "God curse your studies!" if he did not remain at Geneva and assist him in the work of the Reformation?[38] As it was for the introverted Calvin, the weight of the church's call can sometimes feel crushing. Francis Schaeffer said such a call to a reluctant man is like the stamping of metal parts by massive industrial presses. Some men, like Moses and Joshua, have to be "extruded" into leadership.[39]

The call to the ministry of the gospel is an extraordinary call, and the more extraordinary the call, the more extraordinary is the need for confirmation. As the church of Jesus Christ worships and prays and fasts for the forward movement of the kingdom, she should expect at times to be asked to vet for service candidates as unlikely as Paul and at other times to press the same into service (Acts 9:15–16; 13:3).

The gospel ministry requires preaching the Word and shepherding people. One's fitness for those tasks is detected through subjective interests as well as observed giftedness. Ultimately, the work is issued by invitation only, but that call is nonnegotiable when issued by the Spirit internally to a man's soul and externally through the church. The self-confident candidate must be humbled by the overwhelming task to "preach the gospel to all creation" (Mark 16:15) and the reluctant ordinand must remember that, in the end, "the one who calls you is faithful, and he will do it" (1 Thess. 5:24).

NOTES

1 G. Lee Ramsey Jr., *Preachers and Misfits, Prophets and Thieves: The Minister in Southern Fiction* (Louisville: Westminster John Knox, 2008), 6.

2 John Calvin, *Institutes of the Christian Religion*, ed. Ford Lewis Battles (Philadelphia: Westminster Press, 1960), 2.486.

3 Lee, *Preachers and Misfits*, 135.

4 Richard Sibbes, *The Bruised Reed* (Carlisle, PA: Banner of Truth, 1998), 11, 15.

5 *George Whitefield's Journals*, ed. William Wale, (repr., Gainesville, FL: Scholar's Facsimiles and Reprints, 1969), 344.

6 Andrew A. Bonar, *The Biography of Robert Murray McCheyne* (Grand Rapids: Zondervan, 2005), 418.

7 Alexander Whyte, *The Characters in Pilgrim's Progress* (Grand Rapids: Baker, 1979), 262.

8 Joseph Tracy, *The Great Awakening* (Edinburgh: Banner of Truth, 1997), 134–35.

9 Ronald N. Frost, "The Bruised Reed by Richard Sibbes (1577–1635)," in *The Devoted Life: An Introduction to the Puritan Classics*, ed. Kelly Kapic and Randall Gleason (Downers Grove: InterVarsity, 2004), 80.

10 Phillips Brooks, *Lyman Beecher Lectures* (New York: E. P. Dutton, 1877), 77.

11 Donald J. MacNair, *The Practices of a Healthy Church* (Phillipsburg, NJ: P&R Publishing, 1999).

12 Timothy Z. Witmer, *The Shepherd Leader* (Phillipsburg, NJ: P&R Publishing, 2010), 102.

13 Bryan Chapell, *Christ-centered Worship* (Grand Rapids: Baker, 2009), 19–22.

14 Augustine, *Contra Faustum Manicheum*, 19.16, *Nicene and Post-Nicene Fathers of the Christian Church*, ed. Philip Schaaf and Henry Wace, vol. 4 (Grand Rapids: Eerdmans, 1971).
15 *A Sermon Upon Justification* (Philadelphia: B. Franklin, 1741), 28–29.
16 Whyte, *Characters in Pilgrim's Progress*, 140.
17 David Dickson, *The Elder and His Work* (Dallas: Presbyterian Heritage Publications, 1990), 15.
18 Whyte, *Characters in Pilgrim's Progress*, 242.
19 Alexander Whyte, *Lord, Teach Us to Pray* (Vancouver: Regent, 1998), 7.
20 Sally Fitzgerald, ed. *The Habit of Being: The Letters of Flannery O'Connor* (New York: Noonday Press, 1979), 81.
21 Eugene H. Peterson, *Working the Angles: The Shape of Pastoral Integrity* (Grand Rapids: Eerdmans, 1993), 40.
22 John Murray, *Principles of Conduct* (Grand Rapids: Eerdmans, 1957), 240.
23 H. A. Ironside, *Addresses on the Second Epistle to the Corinthians* (New York: Loizeaux, 1939), 133–34.
24 Sermon 188, 2–3, *St. Augustine Sermons for Christmas and Epiphany*, trans. Thomas Comerford Lawler (New York: Newman, 1952), 91–96.
25 Edmund P. Clowney, *Called to the Ministry* (Phillipsburg: P&R, 1964), 30.
26 Clowney, *Called to the Ministry*, 80.
27 As quoted by Adam S. McHugh, *Introverts in the Church* (Downers Grove: IVP, 2009), 115.
28 Jim Collins, *Good to Great and the Social Sectors* (New York: Harper Collins, 2005), 11.
29 L. L. Legters, *The Simplicity of the Spirit-Filled Life* (Farmingdale, NY: Christian Witness Products, 1930), 50.
30 Clowney, *Called to the Ministry*, 83.
31 James Durham, *A Commentary upon the Book of the Revelation* (London: 1658, repr., 2000), 70.
32 Calvin, *Institutes*, 3.16.4.
33 Durham, *Commentary*, 72.
34 Clowney, *Called to the Ministry*, 78–79. Emphasis in the original.
35 *The Book of Church Order: Presbyterian Church in America*, 18–6.
36 Durham, *Commentary*, 75.
37 Ibid.
38 *Commentary on the Psalms* (Grand Rapids: Baker, 1974), xxxvi.
39 "No Little People, No Small Places," in *The Complete Works of Francis A. Schaeffer*, vol. 3 (Westchester: Crossway, 1982), 12–13.

MORE RESOURCES FOR PASTORS FROM P&R

What is Christ's calling to you? You may be seeking an answer, you may be avoiding the question—but when the Lord calls, he will be answered. God's call came suddenly to Elisha, who was plowing a field when Elijah cast the prophet's mantle on him, and to Peter, who was holding a fishing net when Jesus called him.

What does the Bible say about Christ's calling today? We are told that the Lord calls us by name, and every Christian has his or her own calling—a calling as a child of God and a servant of God.

In this timeless book Clowney addresses the question of how the Lord calls us today. Christ's spoken word no longer sounds by the lake of Galilee, but he has not left his disciples without direction.